MW01168441

COLLEGE FOOTBALL'S GREATEST RIVALRIES

NOTRE DAME vs. USC

MATTHEW MONTEVERDE

PowerKiDS press.
New York

For Brian and Meghan

Published in 2013 by The Rosen Publishing Group, Inc.
29 East 21st Street, New York, NY 10010

First Edition

Editors: Dean Galiano and Julie Zerbib
Book Design: Dean Galiano and Julie Zerbib

Photo Credits: Cover, John Mersits/Zuma Press; Back Cover: (top) Gregory Shamus/Getty Images, (bottom) John Pyle/Zuma Press; p. 4 (background photo) Harry How/Getty; Images; p. 5 (background photo) Gregory Shamus/ Getty Images, Collegiate Images/Getty Images; p. 7 Jonathan Daniel/Getty Images; p. 9 Harry How/Getty Images; p. 11 Associated Press; p. 13 George Ling/Getty Images; p. 15 Focus on Sport/Getty Images; p. 17 Tom DiPace/Getty Images; p. 19 John Pyle/Newscom, Todd Rosenberg/Getty Images; pp. 20-21 G.N. Lowrance/Getty Images, IngramPublishing/Newscom; p. 21 (inset) Rick Stewart/Getty Images, (inset) Mike Ehrmann/Getty Images.

Library of Congress Cataloging-in-Publication Data

Monteverde, Matthew.
Notre Dame vs. USC / by Matthew Monteverde. -- 1st ed.
p. cm. -- (College football's greatest rivalries)
Includes index.
ISBN 978-1-4777-1158-3 (library binding) -- ISBN 978-1-4777-1163-7 (pbk.) -- ISBN 978-1-4777-1164-4 (6-pack)
1. Notre Dame--Football--History--Juvenile literature. 2. Notre Dame Fighting Irish (Football team)--History--Juvenile literature. 3. University of Southern California--Football--History--Juvenile literature. 4. University of Southern California Trojans (Football team)--History--Juvenile literature. I. Title.
GV958.M5M66 2013
796.332'630977--dc23

2012042883

Manufactured in the United States of America

CPSIA Compliance Information: Batch #W13PKF: For Further Information contact Rosen Publishing, New York, New York at 1-800-237-9932

CONTENTS

Origins of a Rivalry 4
The Fighting Irish 6
The USC Trojans 8
The Early Years 10
The Comeback 12
Irish Dominance 14
The Trojans Fight On 16
Playing for a Trophy 18
Notre Dame vs. USC Timeline 20
Tale of the Tape 22
Glossary 23
Index 24
Websites 24

ORIGINS OF A RIVALRY

The **rivalry** between the University of Notre Dame and the **University** of Southern California is one of the oldest in college football. It is also one of the most famous rivalries in any US sport. The history between these two football teams dates all the way back to 1926.

Since that 1926 game, Notre Dame and USC have played each other almost every year. The rivalry has produced some of the greatest games in college football history. There is always a lot at stake when the two teams meet. Many times the winner of the matchup has gone on to play for the national championship. At nearly 100 years old, the rivalry between the two schools is just as stong as ever.

Legendary coach Knute Rockne led Notre Dame against USC in the first game between the schools. The teams played a close game. Notre Dame escaped with a one- point win.

THE FIGHTING IRISH

The Notre Dame football team is one of the most popular teams in college football. Nicknamed the Fighting Irish, the team plays its home games at Notre Dame Stadium, in South Bend, Indiana. Although Notre Dame plays in Indiana, the team has fans all over the United States. Notre Dame football fans are so common in fact, that you might know someone who roots for the team. Or you might be a fan yourself.

In addition to being one of the most popular college football teams, Notre Dame is also one of the most successful. Its first season was way back in 1887. Since then, the team has won 11 national championships. It won its most recent championship in 1988. Some notable former Notre Dame football players include Paul Hornung, Joe Montana, and Raghib “The Rocket” Ismail.

Notre Dame linebacker Mante Te'o celebrates after intercepting a pass. The "C" on the front of Te'o's jersey means that he was one of the captains of the football team.

THE USC TROJANS

There is probably no bigger autumn sporting event in Los Angeles, California than a USC football game. The USC football team is known as the **Trojans**. The Trojans are one of the best teams in college football. They play their home games at the Los Angeles Memorial Coliseum. In 1888, USC played its first football game. USC has won 11 national championships during its history.

Some of the best National Football League (NFL) players of all time played football at USC before turning pro. Such players include Marcus Allen, Ronnie Lott, and Reggie Bush. In total, nearly 500 USC players have been selected in the NFL Draft. This is more than any other college. With so many USC players going to the NFL, it's no wonder that the Trojans have won so many championships!

The USC Trojans wear gold and cardinal red uniforms. These have been the school's official colors since 1895.

THE EARLY YEARS

The first football game between Notre Dame and USC was played in 1926. The game was close, but Notre Dame defeated USC by a score of 13-12. On that day, the Notre Dame versus USC rivalry was born.

It didn't take long for the Notre Dame and USC football rivalry to become famous. In 1929, just three years after their first game, the teams played in front of a crowd of more than 112,000 people! There were so many people at the game that it remains one of the most attended games in college football history.

In 1931, USC defeated Notre Dame at South Bend for the first time. The game was a classic! With a minute left in the game, kicker Johnny Baker kicked a 33-yard field goal to give USC the lead. The Trojans held on to win the game 16-14.

Notre Dame and USC battle it out here during the 1931 matchup. USC won the game 16-14. It was USC's first win at South Bend.

THE COMEBACK

One of the most famous games in the rivalry was played in 1974. Notre Dame came into the game as the defending national champions. This means that they had won the championship the year before. When the teams met, USC appeared to be no match for the defending champs.

USC was losing badly. The Trojans found themselves down 24-0 to Notre Dame. The fans at the Los Angeles Memorial Coliseum were so disappointed that they were booing their own team.

USC came to life in a big way, though, and scored an amazing 55 unanswered points! They ended up beating the Irish 55-24. USC then went on to beat Ohio State in the Rose Bowl and win a share of the 1974 national championship.

USC safety Charles Phillips runs after intercepting a pass during the 1974 matchup. Phillips was able to snag three interceptions during the game. His defensive performance was one of the best in the rivalry's long history.

IRISH DOMINANCE

During the 1970s, USC won most of the games in the rivalry. In fact, they lost only two games to Notre Dame during the entire decade. Notre Dame would get their **revenge** in the next decade, though. They did this by winning 11 straight games against the Trojans.

The Notre Dame winning streak began in 1983, when they dominated the Trojans 27-6. Notre Dame did not lose another game against USC until 1996! This win streak remains the longest for either team in the rivalry.

Notre Dame put together some historic teams during the 80s and 90s. The best of them was the 1988 team, which finished the season 12-0 and won the national championship. The championship was the eleventh in the school's history.

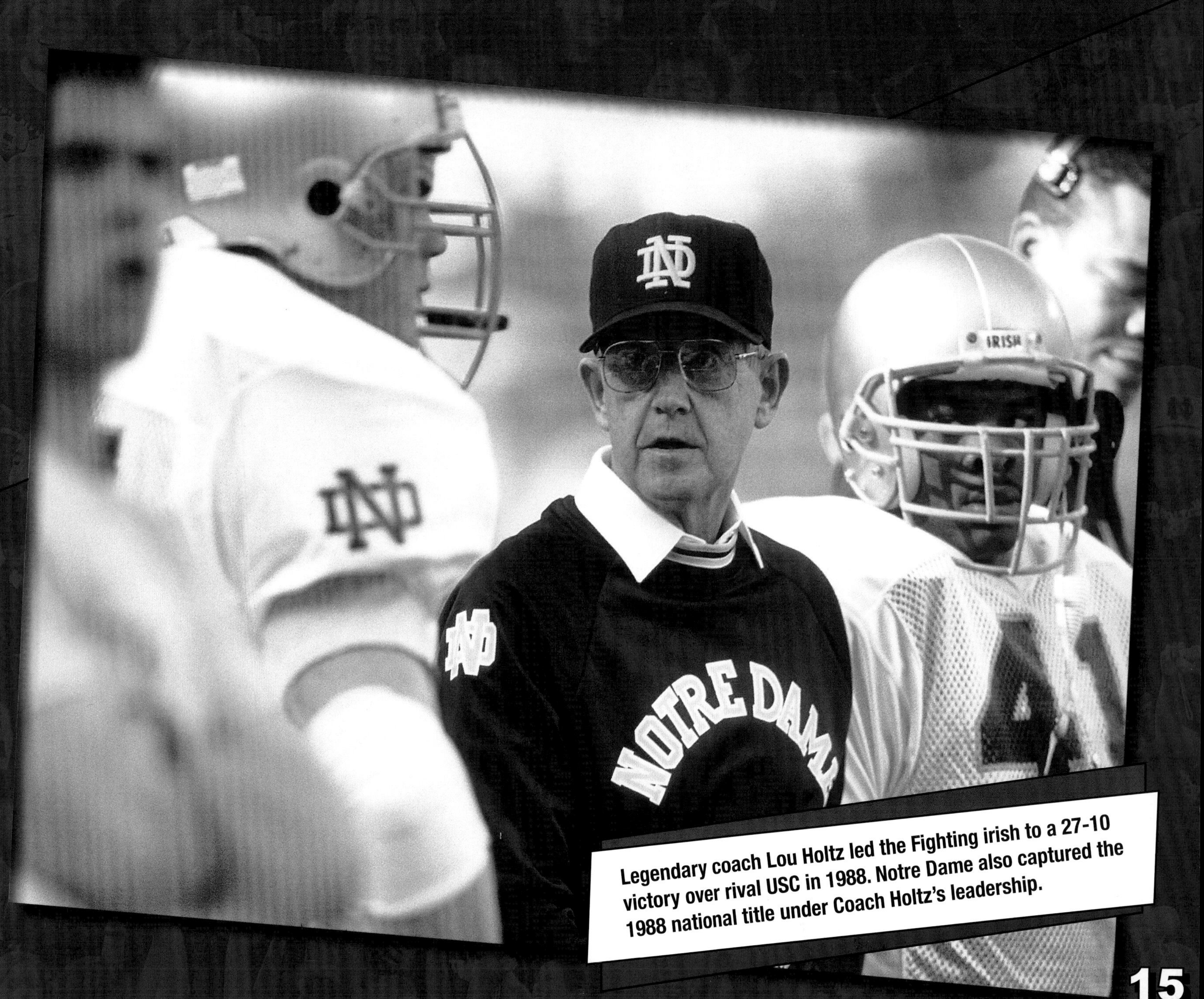

Legendary coach Lou Holtz led the Fighting irish to a 27-10 victory over rival USC in 1988. Notre Dame also captured the 1988 national title under Coach Holtz's leadership.

THE TROJANS FIGHT ON

Notre Dame dominated USC during the 80s and 90s, but USC turned the tide in the 2000s. From 2002 to 2009, USC won eight straight games in the **series**. The USC teams of the 2000s were some of the best in college football. The 2004 team went undefeated and won the national championship.

Perhaps the best USC-Notre Dame game during this period was the 2005 matchup. Defending champion USC was losing 31-28 to Notre Dame late in the fourth quarter. USC had the ball near the Notre Dame end zone, and had time only for one play. USC **quarterback** Matt Leinart took the ball and ran toward the **end zone**. At first, the Notre Dame defense stopped Leinart, but then USC **running back** Reggie Bush pushed Leinart into the end zone for the touchdown. USC beat Notre Dame 34-31, and the play became known as the Bush Push.

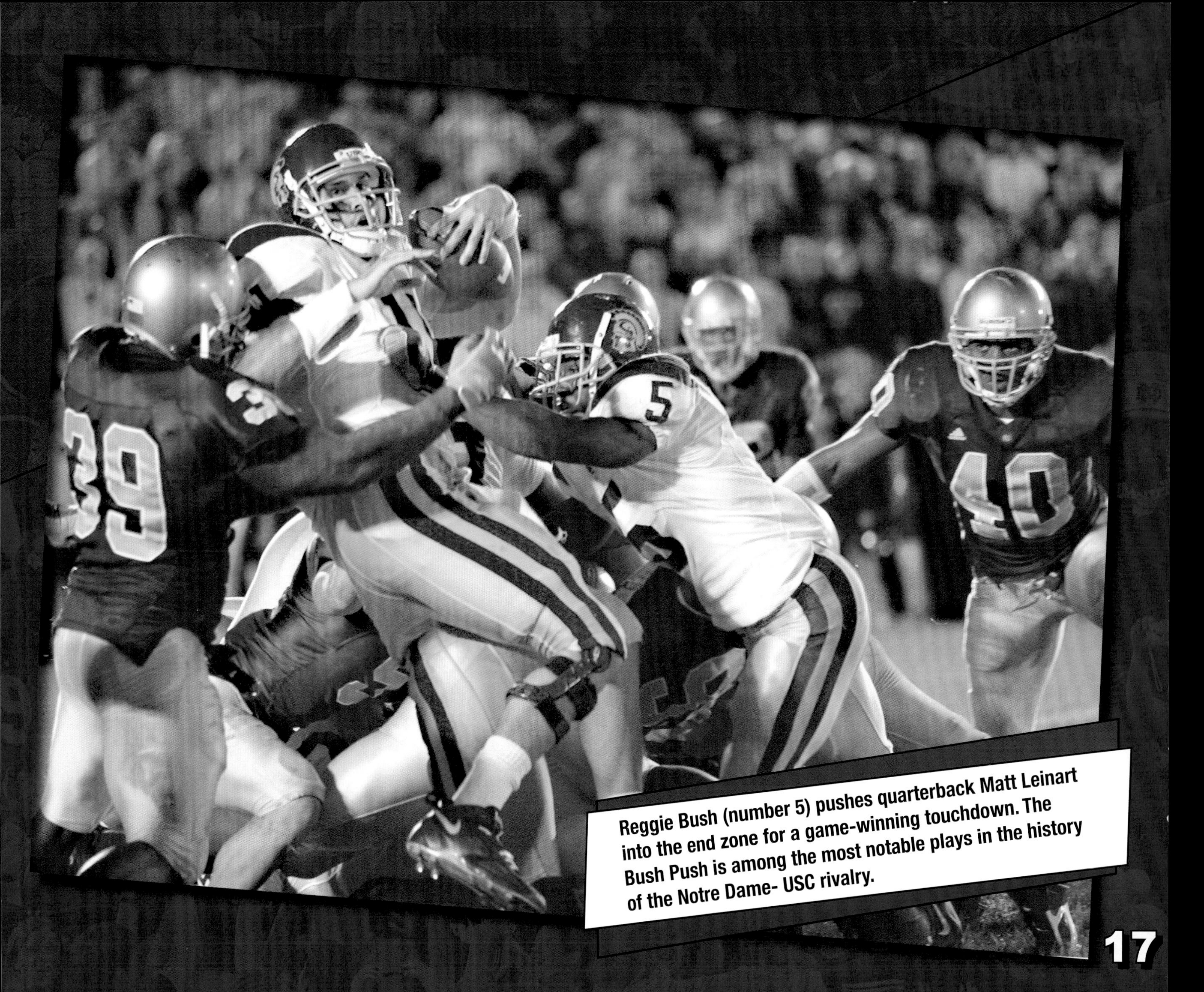

Reggie Bush (number 5) pushes quarterback Matt Leinart into the end zone for a game-winning touchdown. The Bush Push is among the most notable plays in the history of the Notre Dame- USC rivalry.

PLAYING FOR A TROPHY

Each year, the winning team of the USC-Notre Dame matchup is awarded a trophy. The trophy is called the Jeweled Shillelagh. A shillelagh is a type of wooden club or walking stick. The winner of the trophy decorates the trophy with an **ornament**. If Notre Dame wins, they place a shamrock ornament on the trophy. If USC wins, they **decorate** the trophy with a Trojan head ornament.

As you can see, the Notre Dame and USC football rivalry has produced some historic football games. Many college football fans want to know what will happen next in this great rivalry. That's hard to say, but there are sure to be a long line of classic games between Notre Dame and USC in the years to come.

USC has dominated the rivalry in recent years, but Notre Dame was able to take home the Jeweled Shillelagh (inset) after the 2010 game. The Irish won a close game 20-16.

NOTRE DAME vs. USC TIMELINE

1926

Notre Dame and USC meet on the football field for the first time. Notre Dame won the game 13-12.

1966

In the most lopsided victory of the rivalry, Notre Dame shuts out USC 51-0.

1974

USC trails Notre Dame 24-0 late in the second quarter in their home stadium. In a stunning comeback, USC scores 55 points to win the game 55-24.

1983

Notre Dame begins its decade of dominance over USC with a 27-6 victory. The Fighting Irish would not lose again to the Trojans until 1996.

1988

Raghib "The Rocket" Ismail helps lead Notre Dame to the school's eleventh national championship. Notre Dame finished its championship season with a 12-0 record.

2004

Matt Leinart becomes the second USC quarterback to win the Heisman Trophy. It was a good year for the Trojans, as they also took home the BCS National Championship after crushing Oklahoma 55-19, in the Orange Bowl.

TALE OF THE TAPE

NOTRE DAME		USC
South Bend, IN	SCHOOL LOCATION	Los Angeles, CA
1842	UNIVERSITY FOUNDED	1880
80,795	STADIUM CAPACITY	93,607
11	NATIONAL CHAMPIONSHIPS	11
7	HEISMAN WINNERS	7
Notre Dame Leprechaun	MASCOT	Traveler (horse)
Gold and Navy Blue	COLORS	Cardinal and Gold

GLOSSARY

DECORATE (DEH-kuh-Reyt) To furnish or put an ornament on something.

DRAFT (DRAFT) The picking of people for a special purpose.

END ZONE (END zohn) The 10-yard area at each end of a football field where touchdowns are scored.

HALFTIME (HAF-time) A break between the second and third quarters of a football game.

ORNAMENT (OR-nuh-ment) An object used to decorate something.

QUARTERBACK (KWAHR-ter-bak) A player in football who lines up behind the center and directs the offense.

REVENGE (ri-VENJ) The feeling of wanting to defeat a team because of a previous loss.

RIVALRY (RY-vul-ree) Teams that play each other a lot and feel strongly about winning.

RUNNING BACK (RUN-ing BAK) The player on the football field whom the quarterback hands the ball off to.

SERIES (SEIR-eez) a set of sports games played between the same two teams.

TROJANS (TROH-junz) People who were from, or lived in ancient Troy.

UNIVERSITY (yoo-neh-ver-seh-tee) A large school where you can study after high school to earn a degree.

INDEX

A
Allen, Marcus, 8

B
Baker, Johnny, 10
Bush, Reggie, 8

C
championship, 4, 6, 8,12, 14, 16, 21

F
Fighting Irish, 6, 15

H
Hornung, Paul, 6

I
Ismail, Raghib, 6, 21

L
Leinart, Matt, 16, 17
Lott, Ronnie, 8
Los Angeles, 8
Los Angeles Memorial Coliseum, 8, 12

M
Montana, Joe, 6

N
NFL Draft, 8

R
rivalry, 4, 8

S
shillelagh, 18, 19
South Bend, 6, 10, 11
stadium, 6, 20, 22

T
Trophy, 18, 21

U
University of Notre Dame, 4
University of Southern California, 4, 22

WEBSITES

Due to the changing nature of Internet links, PowerKids Press has developed an online list of websites related to the subject of this book. This site is updated regularly. Please use this link to access the list: www.powerkidslinks.com/cfgr/notreusc/